365 Days of Inspiration

Most Emotional and Inspiring Life Changing Quotes for Success, Wealth and Happiness

Wanda Kelly

©Copyright 2022 – *Wanda Kelly* - All rights reserved

The content contained within this book may not be reproduced, duplicated, or transmitted without direct written permission from the author or the publisher.

Under no circumstances will any blame or legal responsibility be held against the publisher, or author, for any damages, reparation, or monetary loss due to the information contained within this book, either directly or indirectly.

Legal Notice

This book is copyright protected. This book is only for personal use. You cannot amend, distribute, sell, use, quote or paraphrase any part, or the content within this book, without the consent of the author-publisher.

Disclaimer Notice

Please note the information contained within this document is for educational and entertainment purposes only. All effort has been executed to present accurate, up to date, and reliable, complete information. No warranties of any kind are declared or implied. Readers acknowledge that the author is not engaging in the rendering of legal, financial, medical, or professional advice.

Table of Contents

Introduction 4

January 5

February 10

March 15

April 22

May 27

June 33

July 38

August 43

September 48

October 53

November 60

December 65

Bonus Quotes 71

Introduction

Inspiration is vital to just about every aspect of our lives, yet it can be elusive. With more technology and devices in our lives than ever before, it's easy to get distracted, to remain insatiably busy, and to lose touch with our inspiration. If we aren't mindful, we can get caught up in the drama, negativity, and hyper pace of the world in which we live. These simple, but powerful, quotes can help open your mind and heart and remind you what truly matters in life, which is no small thing.

Life is never constant; it is a bumpy ride which sometimes takes us to our lowest points. That is the time when most of us lose hope and determination. To regain our inner strength and confidence, we often need to look and learn from past and present examples. Men and women with exemplary characteristics have shown the world how to win true peace, contentment, and real success in life. Where their deeds set an example for all, their words have left indelible marks on people's minds and spirits. Those pearls of inspiration have guided many different individuals to become an inspiration themselves.

January

Sometimes you wake up. Sometimes the fall kills you. And sometimes, when you fall, you fly.
— Neil Gaiman

***

Hold fast to dreams,
For if dreams die
Life is a broken-winged bird,
That cannot fly.
— Langston Hughes

***

The unexamined life is not worth living.
— Socrates

***

Look what happens with
A love like that,
It lights the Whole Sky.
— Hafiz

****

A person of infinite variety might spend a lifetime and never find another person exactly like himself, yet hundreds of thousands of men must die daily, their probations are a barrenness of experience, because there is not one there for them to meet. ~ Robert Louis Stevenson

***

There is a great difference between being restless and being active. ~ Aeschylus

***

A real education does not teach you what to think, but how to think. ~ Benjamin Franklin

***

My sole foundation is penance and prayer. ~ Saint Catherine of Siena

***

Life is a dead thing, and nothing works better to help a fellow to forget it than to be dead drunk most of his time. ~ Will Rogers

***

To want friendship is a great fault. — Confucius

***

What is woven with love, will be woven in love. — Rumi

***

Wealth being very scanty at the time, his clothes were very plain and coarse. — Benjamin Franklin

***

The wise man thinks himself rich when he has what he needs; the poor man when he has what he wants. —Unknown

***

If I had to choose between the things I have done and the stuff of my dreams, I would choose the latter. — Albert Einstein

And life is neither happiness nor pain, but somehow both. — Ivan Turgenev

***

Life is only a series of natural events, each of which alone would be insignificant. But multiplied together, they form a chain of consequences; and thus, in every important chain are found the links which bind human action and affect it. — Benjamin Disraeli

***

Be tolerant toward others. Set an example. Of course the world is imperfect. — H. Jackson Brown, Jr.

***

I am grateful for the day, because it has given me the experience of a lifetime. — Bill Gates

***

"Live each day to its fullest. Make your dreams a reality. Take chances, be willing to fail. Don't be afraid of what some people in a position of power will think of you. Be true to yourself. Have a sense of humor. Love and enjoy life." — Steve Wozniak, co-founder of Apple Inc.

***

Work gives you things. Play gives you fun. — Neil Young

***

"Well, I'll be honest, like most people these days. I don't have any idea what I want to do. And then, I don't know why I do what I do. But people have asked me why I do what I do. And I've answered them. And I want to do it anyway. So... hey. Why not? Give it a shot." — Elliot — Arrested Development (2001)

***

Most of the great problems of the world are caused by people's opinions. — Benjamin Disraeli

***

"If you spend much time in nature, it will change you." — H. Jackson Brown, Jr.

***

Life is a series of lessons, not school. — Gabriel García Márquez

***

Love is the absence of judgment.
 — Dalai Lama XIV

***

Attitude is a choice. Happiness is a choice. Optimism is a choice. Kindness is a choice. Giving is a choice. Respect is a choice. Whatever choice you make makes you. Choose wisely.
 — Roy T. Bennett

***

"If you can't make a mistake you can't make anything." - Marva Collin

****

"If we wait until we're ready, we'll be waiting for the rest of our lives." - Lemony Snicket

****

"Don't give up, don't take anything personally, and don't take no for an answer." - Sophia Amoruso

****

"The person who starts simply with the idea of getting rich won't succeed; you must have a larger ambition." - John D. Rockefeller
"No matter what information you have, no matter what you are doing, you can be wrong." - Larry Hite
"Forget your excuses. You either want it bad or don't want it at all." – Anonymous

****

"So the bottom line is this: You've got to think for yourself and decide what is relevant to you and what's noise (no one can do it for you)." – Anonymous

****

February

***

The division of mankind into patrials, nations, and tribes is founded in human nature itself. — Jean-Jacques Rousseau

***

It is the custom of nations to submit to their bastions upon occasion. — Jean-Jacques Rousseau

***

Clouds may gather over the earth, but an opportunity is always present; it is but a question of the mood in which you see it. — Alexis Carrel

***

What you think depends upon what you know. — W. H. Murray

***

You are not your circumstances (though you are who you are while you are living in those circumstances). You are who you choose to be. — Barbara De Angelis

***

Suffering is better than pleasure. — Lao Tzu

***

We do not remember the pleasures, but the pains. — Plutarch

***

It is not enough to have a good future; it is necessary also to know how to prepare for it. — Vygotsky

***

Knowledge is never enough for a mind thirsty for more. — Robert Louis Stevenson

***

The true knowledge of the world is to see it as it is, not as you want it to be. — Alexander The Great

***

A man of 1000 cuts never dies. — Unknown

***

Believe you can and you're halfway there. — Theodore Roosevelt

***

For it is not things which are seen, but the things which are not seen, which are worth preserving. — Plutarch

***

The dream of a body without illness, is only a dream. Wishful dreaming is too feeble to bring a cure. — Aristotle

***

Challenge your limits and prove that everyone has the power to create their own future. — Les Brown

***

Success is the progressive achievement of worthy goals. — William Feather

***

The ideal of work is life in the fullest sense. — Emerson

***

Life is a great revelation. ~ Husserl

***

If we are earning all the money we should be earning, that does not make us any more than half great. ~ Michael McNicholas

***

It's damn difficult being anyone but me. It's damn difficult being any one else. ~ Ebenezer Scrooge

***

Uncomplicated living doesn't last long. Uncomplicated thinking has to be replaced by complicated thinking. ~ Nelson Riddle

***

It's difficult for me to write, I'm thinking and feeling all the time about things other than what I'm writing. That can be a very attractive quality in a woman. ~ James M. Cain

***

What you do speaks so loudly ... that I cannot hear what you say. ~ Louis Armstrong

***

In your anger, you make a mistake; in your favor you make an opportunity. ~ The Prince

***

It's generally a mistake to be a second rate political thinker, but there's no danger of that in government. ~ Doug Christie

***

There could be a time when the press would not be free to criticize the government in a way that we all believe is essential. ~ Thomas Jefferson

***

A claim to ignorance is an excuse for being so. ~ W. Somerset Maugham

***

Greed is our master, friendship and gratitude our slaves. ~ Jean Marie Guyau

***

Crime is the dividend of repression. ~ Nelson Mandela

***

All the best tales start at home. ~ H.P. Lovecraft

***

We must think and live on our own. ~ Charles de Gaulle

March

***

Instead of talking about what you want in life why not focus on wanting what you have? ~ Mike McNicholas

If you do not accept the things of this world, you will not recognize them. If you do not recognize them, you will not believe in them. ~ Jean de La Fontaine

***

Man is a god in the making. ~ Rumi

***

The life of his existence is a miracle that is blessed and immortal. ~ Rabindranath Tagore

***

If you have the courage, all obstacles become steps. ~ Lamartine

***

I've always thought it was a very good idea to teach people how to think and not what to think. ~ Richard M. Nixon

***

The first step is to bring down the wrath of divine justice upon the oppressors. After that, all men will be able to enjoy the reign of peace untroubled. ~ Wang Yangming

To write about love is to make a bag in which to gather up all the kernel of kindness and all of the sweetness we have garnered from the summer of life. It is to create a vessel in which to hold the always too scattered fruits of a soul which is ever so ready to scatter them. ~ Antoine de Saint-Exupery

***

Turn your wounds into wisdom. ~ Oprah Winfrey

***

The soul is a continuous creation which is never fully manifest in the deeds of the body. ~ Professor Tybalt

***

God, if I could have dreamed of her becoming as she is, I would have turned back time to gather, to restore, to save what I had let go in my wayward dreams of possibilities. ~ Chrystos, "Infinite Space, Infinite God"

***

A nation constantly at war is no longer a nation but a decaying corpse full of maggots. Every nation that lives by war lives in a state of chronic fear. ~ Dr. Henry Kissinger
***

When you play a sport, you want to be as good as you can be. Of course, everybody does. ~ Gracie Gold

***

The trophies I earned over the years, I really cherish. Various awards. But I've also been very fortunate to win in a lot of other ways. I've been very fortunate to be able to speak at various conventions and share my story with millions of people. And it's given me the chance to see how accessible and responsive I am. I've been able to go to people who would otherwise never hear me speak and to teach a few people, who then had a chance to have a greater experience. I'm still very grateful for that. -~ Maren Morris

***

Let us not forget that our personal triumphs are also the triumphs of our fellow men. ~ Byron Nelson

***

How you treat people is your karma, your representation of what you deserve. ~ Gershom Scholem

***

They're with us at their very best when they're playing. ~ Joe North

***

Do what you like; you'll like what you do. ~ Adina Apartment

***

Never bend your head. Always carry it straight forward. Never make excuses. Never try to explain. Always try to go one better. Never stop reaching for the stars. ~ David L. Lawrence

***

Records are made to be broken. ~ Roger Bannister

***

The moment when one decides to live is the moment when one is truly born. ~ Jean Anouilh

***

There is only one success in life possible, to be able to spend one's life in his own way. ~ Arthur Schopenhauer

***

People's moods rise and fall, but the sun rises and sets. ~ Elbert Hubbard

***

I believe that all things happen for a reason, and when it seems as if things are out of control, God steps in and sees to it that everything turns out for the best. ~ C. Robin Cook

***

Time heals all wounds in a process of reincarnation. ~ Toni Morrison

***

God creates the future; you create the past; the future you have created is what governs the present. ~ C.S. Lewis

***

When my father was young, he was told, "Go to college." So he did. When his father was young, he was told, "Go to college." So he did. Now, my son is being told, "Go to college." ~ Jewel

***

I'm obviously not an expert on communication but, after long consideration, I decided to write down my creed, which I hold to be true for all time and for all men. ~ David H. Lawrence

***

When your time comes, the time will come. ~ William Shakespeare

***

The only real valuable things are valuable only because they are rare. Common things are cheap. Water is water. ~ Henry Miller
****
The man who seeks to be his own law is swift to anger, slow to know himself, and at war with the world. ~ Solomon

***

Wisdom is the only wealth. ~ Omar Khayyám

***

A living thing is never really dead; nor is a dead thing really living. We think of things badly. ~ Oscar Wilde

***

I do not know very much; I am a very retiring person. But I do know this. I wish to speak. ~ Thucydides

***

Laws do not restrain the wicked or protect the weak. Men in authority will always do their best to make life miserable for others. It is in the nature of men to hate. And all history is written in blood. ~ Dan Simmons, "Carrion Comfort"

***

History is philosophy teaching by examples. ~ Jose Ortega y Gasset

***

Always remember, you are unique. Just like everyone else. ~ Dieter Hildebrandt

***

I love humanity as much as any psychopath. ~ Friedrich Nietzsche

***

You can always tell a fanatic. He'll have the face of a saint and the heart of a devil. ~ Sigmund Freud

***

The greatest glory in living lies in never cease to strive. ~ Frederick Douglass

***

Patience is the parent of success. ~ Thomas Carlyle (author of "Rousseau, Hero of Solitude)"

***

The sufferer I, but never my soap. ~ Othello

***

Life is a game and anything less than a game is not life. ~ Charles Lindberg

April

***

Investment in people is the highest form of investment there is. ~ Lincoln Barnett

***

"You are responsible for your life" is a lie. No, you aren't. No, you aren't. I had an epiphany while I was stealing from K-Mart, and realized the truth. The truth is that society is responsible for your life. Society is responsible for your life. ~ Jewel

***

Nobody has listened carefully to what I actually said. i said, "I like talking about myself." Excuse me, but what does that mean? Did I say less than twenty words a day? Did I talk about myself more than anybody else? All I said was, "I like talking about myself." ~ David H. Lawrence

***

There is a little shop on wheels. It contains a golden statue of Buddha with one hand pointing to the sky and the other pointing toward the earth. There is a golden statue of Jesus with both hands raised into the air. There is a statue of Mohammed, with his eyes closed and his hands raised into the air. There are also dozens of smaller statues, all of them pointing a different way. One of these old statues had a muffler. Another was missing a hand. ~ Jewel

***

Nothing worth having comes easily. ~ Napoleon Hill

***

The moments we enjoy wasting are not wasted. ~ A. B. Curtis

***

Fame, like most other things in life, is easier earned than enjoyed. ~ Frank Capra

***

The weakest man alive can never be so strong as when he surrenders to the temptation to be morally superior. ~ C. S. Lewis

***

You have been given a great gift. You were given the ability to think. Let that be your power, your might, your magic. Your pain when you walk the Way will be spiritual through your mind, not through your body. ~ David H. Lawrence

***

The will may be weak, but the imagination makes up for it. ~ Luigi Pirandello

***

To die will be an awfully big adventure. ~ A.A. Milne

***

To reach the goal you must plan the journey. ~ John C. Maxwell

***

When I give a dinner party, it's not always easy to tell who I'm really serving, the guests or the food. ~ Grace Coddington

***

I've often heard it said that all great achievements are due to luck. Horseshoes and horseshoes. It takes two to make a thing go right. If you're the person that doesn't get the break, I'm the one who will. I'm the one who will while you're the one who won't.~ Michael Reagan

***

I hear and I forget. I see and I remember. I do and I understand.~ Confucius

***

Glory is fleeting but obscurity is forever.~ Douglas Adams

***

There is nothing more pathetic than a successful person who feels he has nothing more to learn. ~ Thornton Wilder

***

What's the use of having beauty without brains? ~ Dale Carnegie

***

Doing something wrong doesn't decide who you are; misunderstanding does. ~ Whitney Powell

***

What happens between us is never anyone else's responsibility but ours alone in our own way. ~ Toni Morrison

***

I know a woman who's very, very old and can't hear or see or speak. She can only stare into space. She was born in the mid-19th century and she grew older and older and older and older and older, and nothing much else happened. Her name was Charlotte. Now, Charlotte didn't realize she was old, but everyone else in the nursing home knew she was very, very old. ~ Jewel

***

I breathe through my eyes. ~ Suzume

***

Three things of life don't stay in your body: lies, dreams, and desires. ~ Kevin Macdonald

***

Sometimes it's hard for people to admit they're wrong or have made a mistake. ~ Kevin O'Leary
****
What we are today comes from our thoughts of the past. Our actions in the present are influenced by our memory of the past, and our expected future. ~ Julius Daugherty

***

There is no more powerful weapon in the hands of the oppressor than the brain of the oppressed. What he really needed was an education. The consciousness of his own self-worth may be all that is needed to lift him from his half-conscious, servile relationship to the world at large. ~ William W. Turner

***

Wealth can be lost in a moment of folly, health in a day of indolence, character in an hour of naughty behavior, and honor in a minute of midnight deliberation. ~ A.E.Arnold

***

I'm not an angel, but I'm not some demon either. I was just one of the guys who got caught. I have regrets, but I am not ashamed of myself. ~ Bo Doggett

***

Life is pain and unfairness, yet you can't stop living because you're afraid of pain. ~ E.E.Cummings

***

I am not arguing for the collective amnesiaof the human race. ~ John Kenneth Galbraith

***

The sincere individual thinks his life is important - he has to protect the value of it. He has to stick to his ideals. They are not just recreational, they are of great worth and permanent importance. He is like a tree that puts all its roots firmly in the materal earth. ~ Erich Fromm

May

***

One can't find one's true love by looking for it. One must first look within. ~ Groucho Marx

***

Stepping back from your own life and taking another look at it might help you see the emptiness of your contentment. ~ Susan Ertz

***

Anyone can become a millionaire. But earning that kind of money takes more than just clocking in every day, it also takes a desire to be wealthy beyond reason. ~ Kevin O'Leary

***

It isn't the minds we teach, but those we reach, that matter most in education. ~ Adina Apartment

***

The more you go through life, the more you realize that everything is basically just a big circle that we are all just trying to get back to.~ Sunny Wayne

***

To know someone deeply in one lifetime may take seventy years; to know everyone, a thousand lifetimes. ~ Lao Tzu

***

It is the nature of living creatures to have the urge to move, to change, and to grow. ~ Paul Hawken

***

Everyone has beauty but not everyone sees it. ~ Bernardino De Sahagun

***

I have learned not to look back unless I'm planning to go that way. ~ Robert Frost

***

If I could choose my last words, that would be it: "Doaa."~ Doaa El-Zoghbi

***

The sea is at our feet, we're looking at the world askew. ~ Grace Coddington

***

I've got enough love to give you everything I've ever got; if you like, I'll give it to you again. ~ William Blake

***

I'm not an expert on avoiding mistakes. i'm an expert on making mistakes and getting up after I'm knocked down. ~ Robert A. Heinlein

***

You can keep those negative thoughts out of your head by filling it up with positive ones. ~ Joe Vitale

***

If you think about the good things, the good things will happen to you. ~ Michael McNicholas

***

Literature is news that stays news. ~ Joseph Brodsky

***

Save your strength for the hills. ~ Dean Karnazes
***

When you open your eyes to this moment, this is when your life starts to become significant. This is when you will find your gift, your talent, your passion, and your profession. This is where you will meet your greatest challenges, and this is where your life will be transformed. ~ Anne Schraff

***

Commitment is the only way you can achieve what you want. It's the only way you can give your full and undivided attention to the challenge at hand... We know from experience that our ideas produce only humble beginnings, but the great challenges require a greater sense of conviction. It's our commitment to our ideas that allows us to break through. [On transforming a startup idea into a startup company]

***

If you don't know what you're fighting for, you can never win. ~ Michael Alago

***

I have spent the night thinking about it. It is hard and frustrating not to win. But I am a positive thinking guy. I do not define myself by wins or losses. I define myself by how close I get to my goals. [On his team's loss on Survivor: Gabon]

***

It is something like the taste of a potato. ~ J.B. Priestly

***

If you don't know what you're fighting for, you'd better be fighting for something. ~ Michael Alago

***

We are all produced by what we think. We are shaped by what we think, even if what we think is only a dream. ~ Ellen Key

***

The worst lesson that I have learned over the years is complacency in the face of injustice. I have been hurt because of it... This is a great reflection on my part to not be more involved in the protection of human rights in Ghana. I have not been able to protect my own rights, therefore how can I protect the rights of Ghanaians? ~ Edem Haddy

***

The rule of the many is not wise. The love of the many is not quickly won. Love of the few is more enduring. ~ Joseph D. Welch

***

I've been very clear that this is a brawl. It's going to be a little bit like Rocky. - Rex Ryan on the Jets and Bills preseason game

***

Life can be simple, but it requires a lot of simplicity. ~ Michael Levenson

***

You don't get things done in this world by thinking like the people you are chasing after. ~ Peter F. Drucker

***

I would rather be a camel than live the life of a classically trained musician. Perhaps it's because I was one of a kind. Perhaps it's because I've seen people who truly "love" music, and I've seen that love smother their talent. ~ Ani DiFranco

***

The present gives birth to the future. ~ Leonardo da Vinci

***

We live in a world that has lost its way. We have to reinvent our lives from the ground up. Start again. If this were easy to do, if this were as easy as it seems to say, we would have done this already. ~ Pico Iyer

***

When I paint a picture, I start at the top and work down. When you start at the bottom, you're always having to stop and color your way up. ~ Roy Lichtenstein

June

***

The main thing to be careful about is not to take any one merit too seriously, for fear of the others getting neglected. ~ J. B. Priestley

***

I was accused of being a black militant. I wasn't a black militant. I was a Martin Luther King militant. I didn't have a black mind; I had a human mind. ~ Abraham Bolden

***

A man who doesn't know what he wants is a man who needs help. ~ Ella Wheeler Wilcox

***

Greatness is a prescription for a life that is richer, nobler, and more interesting than the one that comes from having nothing inside you that wants to get out. ~ Daniel J. Creedon

***

What we are is God's gift to us. What we do with it is up to us. ~ Marilyn vos Savant

***

It is not our duty to teach the world; it is our duty to help the world discover what it has always had within it. ~ José Ortega y Gasset

Be careful in your interpretations, for in life, the opportunities which promise the most are often the worst. ~ William J. Kavanagh

***

I'm a pushover. I give up. I give up very easily. That's why I have so many friends...so many wonderful friends. ~ Jonathan Winters

***

I'm very direct. I can't stand anything that isn't totally clear. I'm not interested in anything vague. I don't mean to be offensive, but in my head everything is either black or white. ~ Arthur Rubinstein

***

The future, we are told, belongs to those who can see far enough to reach out and take it. ~ Laurence J. Peter

***

Sow a thought, reap an action. Actions reap seeds, seeds sow new actions. May this propagate endlessly. ~ R. P. Blackmore

***

All human endeavor can be traced back to discovering a way to make something work that wasn't working before. ~ Fred Kofman

***

If you don't ask, you don't get. ~ Jon Varvatos

***

What is most important in life? To be what you are in reality, at least one day. ~ Søren Kierkegaard

***

Today is a very special day, because one day, a long time ago, I gave birth to you. ~ Marcus Mumford

****

You can make of life what you will. ~ Lucinda Williams

***

To be proud of one's faults is a condition of being wise. ~ Mark Twain

***

There is no arguing with the stubborn, but there is no responding to the insane. ~ R. P. Blackmore

***

You've got to be ready for whatever life throws at you. ~ Dave Grohl

***

As a child I had a number of advantages that no amount of talent or ability at any other time could have gained me. For the first seven years, I was merely a baby. ~ Mark Twain

***

Anyone who can make a salad only makes a mess of the kitchen floor. ~ Mark Twain

***

Nothing whatsoever worth doing has ever succeeded without enthusiasm. ~ Edith Wharton

***

You can never know everything, but it is not hard to have a good idea of what the world is like. ~ Iain M Banks

***

Expect the best. Prepare for the worst. Capitalize on what comes. ~ Heraclitus

***

The greatest thing you'll ever learn is just to love and be loved in return. ~ Elton John

***

Each day brings new choices. your choices are the key to success. ~ Denis Waitley

***

It doesn't matter what happens to the ship if the oars continue to beat the water ! ~ Sidney Sheldon

***

Nothing is impossible, but the first to expect it, may be out of date. ~ Edmond Rostand

***

Every morning in every way it's a brand new day. ~ R. N. Davidson

***

No one's perfect. Not me, not you, not the President. ~ Ann Richards

***

If you think it's hard to be a woman, try being a man. ~ Robert A. Heinlein

***

Respect for anyone should begin with oneself and extend outward ever so slowly. ~ Robert A. Heinlein

July

***

Where few words are, bold deeds take place. ~ Robert A. Heinlein

***

To be eccentric in opinion, and to have no desire to change it, is a sign of good breeding. ~ Robert A. Heinlein

***

A curious thing never fails to amaze me. People will lie and cheat and steal from others without hesitation if it is to their advantage. Yet if they lose merely one dollar by it, they will agonize for days that they have behaved so badly. ~ Robert A. Heinlein

***

Failure is impossible. ~ Robert A. Heinlein

***

We have to believe in free will. But the worst of it is, no matter how careful you are, how sensible you are, you are going to make mistakes. ~ Robert A. Heinlein

***

There is nothing to writing. All you do is sit down at a typewriter and bleed. ~ Robert A. Heinlein

***

I find that any sufficiently advanced technology is indistinguishable from magic. ~ Arthur C. Clarke

***

It is not Always possible to Be a saint. ~ Robert A. Heinlein

***

Life is a series of natural miracles, a sequence of random propositions, a creature of constant change. ~ Robert A. Heinlein

***

Always start at the top; work down. Always. ~ Robert A. Heinlein

***

You can't wait for inspiration. You have to go after it with a club. ~ Jack London

***

Happiness is a way station between too little and too much. ~ Robert A. Heinlein

***

We will only find the important answers to our questions if we continue to ask them. ~ Robert A. Heinlein

***

If you aren't living on the edge, you're taking up too much room. ~ Robert A. Heinlein

Today's computer systems are based on deodorant design. ~ Robert A. Heinlein

***

Only those who will risk going too far can possibly find out how far one can go. ~ Robert A. Heinlein

***

We wanted him to be S.T.E.A.M. – six dimensions, the ultimate in man. ~ Robert A. Heinlein

***

In science-fiction, there are no rules. In science-fiction, anything is possible. ~ Robert A. Heinlein

***

Given a large enough time in advance, any problem can be solved in the worst possible way. ~ Robert A. Heinlein

***

It is more fun to talk with someone who doesn't use long, difficult words but rather short, easy words like "What about lunch?" ~ Robert A. Heinlein

***

The is one word I never want to hear again. That word is 'prejudice. ~ Robert A. Heinlein

***

Let's face it, astronauts are pretty big suckers for pretty women ~ Robert A. Heinlein

***

Any sufficiently advanced technology is indistinguishable from magic. ~ Arthur C. Clarke

***

Grown-ups would rather die than think. ~ Robert A. Heinlein

***

Life is short. Break the rules. ~ Robert A. Heinlein

***

I often think that the ancients were wonderfully insightful about the human condition. They created this world, and they understood it so well that they produced symbols of all the things it could possibly mean to be human. ~ Robert A. Heinlein

***

It is perhaps the infinite detail of possible states that constitutes the scary part of the universe. ~ Robert A. Heinlein

***

Every good scientist is also a good myth maker. ~ Robert A. Heinlein

***

It's not what we have in life, it's what we do with what we have. ~ Michael McNicholas

****

It is amazing how much can be done if no one cares who gets the credit. ~ Anonymous ~

****

We can't become what we need to be by remaining what we are. ~ Henry David Thoreau ~

*****

"It's not what happens to you in life that matters. It's what you do about it that really counts. ~ Henry David Thoreau ~

*****

Do not be forever clasping your pearls to your bosom when you might be using them of to serve somebody else. ~ Golda Meir ~

August

Don't be too aggressive. Relax and be yourself and let the chips fall where they may. ~ Michael McNicholas

****

You have to carve the fireplace with the greatest care, but once you've done it you don't think about it again. ~ Michael McNicholas

****

Everything that is great and remarkable in the world has been accomplished by people who have dared to be themselves. ~ Michael McNicholas

***

Make up your mind to turn the tables and play the game. ~ Ernest Hemingway ~

****

If you do not move forward the others will pass you by. ~ Michael McNicholas

****

If you don't like something stop doing it and then change it. ~ Michael McNicholas

****

You have to make the best of each and every moment in life, because in the blink of an eye it can be over. ~ Michael McNicholas

****

It is amazing how much can be done if no one cares who gets the credit. ~ Anonymous ~

****

No matter what happens, the important thing is that no one forgets. ~ Michael McNicholas

****

Do not worry about the future, or what may never be, but focus entirely on the present moment. ~ Alan Lakein ~

****

Stop me if you've heard this one before, the world is divided into cats who play well with others and cats who do not. I'm here to say that there's a remedy — do not play with others, you'll lose. ~ Michael McNicholas

****

If you don't want to be found do not get found. ~ Michael McNicholas

****

Your mission in life is to be, after receiving all you are capable of receiving, a blameless steward of that which remains. ~ Michael McNicholas

****

Do as you would be done by. ~ Michael McNicholas

****

Sexual harassment doesn't start with a complaint; it starts with a wink. ~ Michael McNicholas

***

When one door closes another door opens. ~ Douglas Adams ~

***

The way that people speak about themselves is often the way that they feel themselves to be. ~ Michael McNicholas

****

When it comes to the very best things in life, you have to take the time to earn them. ~ Michael McNicholas

****

When I am trying to achieve something of great importance to me, the first thing I do in the morning is tie up all the loose ends that are there. ~ Charles Schwab ~

****

People who are mindful all day long will be inclined to be mindful every minute of the day. ~ Michael McNicholas

****

It is not what happens to you in life that matters. It is what you do about it that really counts. ~ Henry David Thoreau ~

****

Looking at things too long is not the way to investigate them. ~ Henry David Thoreau ~

****

A man is known by the company he keeps. ~ Joseph Andrews ~

****

Fail often, fail often; fail better! ~ Michael McNicholas

****

Some people are ready to be free some people are ready to be free from themselves some people are not ready to be free ~ Michael McNicholas

****

A few per cent of the universe is ours to look after and it would be a pity if they let slip the opportunity. ~ Michael McNicholas

****

In matters of style, swim with the current; in matters of principle, stand like a rock. ~ Thomas Jefferson ~

****

The mind is like a parachute, it functions only when it is open. ~ Thomas Jefferson ~

****

We get to choose the way that we react to the events that happen to us. ~ Michael McNicholas

****

A commitment to something greater than self is a necessary piece of freedom. ~ Anonymous ~

****

The thing that lies at the foundation of positive thinking is the fact that you are going to do the best you can under the circumstances. ~ Michael McNicholas

****

If you are unnecessarily hard on yourself, people around you are unnecessarily hard on you. ~ Michael McNicholas

****

The greatest tragedy is not to die, but to feel that you have lived and lived for nothing. ~ Francois de La Rochefoucauld ~

****

September

There's always a bright side, even to the worst tragedy. ~ Michael McNicholas

****

Success is a poor man's refuge when the world mistakes him for being proud. ~ Michael McNicholas

****

The surest way to be content is to wish for what you have, is to wish to be content. For the secret of freedom lies in some such foolishness as that. We are all born of kings and beggars alike. ~ Henry Wadsworth Longfellow ~

****

Freedom is never assured it has to be chosen every day. ~ Michael McNicholas

****

A man is known by the company he keeps. ~ Joseph Andrews ~

****

The thing that lies at the foundation of positive thinking is the fact that you are going to do the best you can under the circumstances. ~ Michael McNicholas

****

A few per cent of the universe is ours to look after and it would be a pity if they let slip the opportunity. ~ Michael McNicholas

****

When everything seems to be going against you, remember that the airplane takes off against the wind, not with it. ~ Henry Ford ~

****

Freedom is never assured it has to be chosen every day. ~ Michael McNicholas

****

To enjoy the fruit of success you must first sow the seeds of determination. ~ Gregory H. Whitman ~

****

It is not what others get out of you, but what you get out of the experience that counts. ~ Harry Browne ~

****

Be more concerned with your character than with your reputation, because your character is what you really are, while your reputation is merely what others think you are. ~ Colin Cowherd ~

****

Reactions count for more than actions. ~ Colin Cowherd ~

****

You cannot climb a ladder unless you are willing to climb for the purpose of climbing the ladder. ~ Anthony J. D'Angelo ~

*****

You are the person who you think you are, not the person others think you are. ~ Michael McNicholas

****

You may receive from others what they do to you, but you cannot give to others what they do not have in themselves. ~ Michael McNicholas

****

A bad man is a man without a heart. ~ Michael McNicholas

****

Hurry and use the moments which are given to you. ~ Michael McNicholas

****

If you are not free to have a good time, you may as well go home. ~ Michael McNicholas

****

The most certain sign of good times is the ability to say No. ~ Michael McNicholas

****

The longest journey begins with a single step. ~ Michael McNicholas

****

Answer a fool according to his folly, lest he be wise in his own eyes. ~ Proverbs 26:5 ~

****

A heart that acts as a brake on the feet is bound to be trampled. ~ Michael McNicholas

****

Life is what happens while you are busy making other plans. ~ John Lennon ~

****

To die without having enjoyed prosperity is the greatest mischance Death can deal us. ~ Michael McNicholas

****

If you don't always do those things for others that you should do for yourselves, you'll find that the time never comes when you can do anything for yourself. ~ Michael McNicholas

****

Nothing great is ever achieved without enthusiasm. ~ Michael McNicholas

****

It's only by taking risks that we find out if we are really free. ~ Michael McNicholas

****

Freedom is never assured it has to be chosen every day. ~ Michael McNicholas

****

When it all comes down to it, who you are is way more important than what you have. ~ Michael McNicholas

****

Freedom is on a long road; our hope is to cut down that road to a distance we can all travel easily. ~ Michael McNicholas

****

You may receive from others what they do to you, but you cannot give to others what they do not have in themselves. ~ Michael McNicholas

****

Sow an action, reap a habit. ~ Michael McNicholas

****

A lot of people only begrudgingly experience their happiness. ~ Michael McNicholas

October

It is easy to climb Mount Everest, it is not easy to climb your Everest. ~ Robin Sharma

***

There is nothing you can't accomplish if you're willing to sacrifice the awards and praises of the world for your true reward. ~ Kevin Kruse

***

I think the scariest moment is always just before you start. ~ Stephen King

***

Some people are ready to be free some people are ready to be free from themselves some people are not ready to be free ~ Michael McNicholas

****

The most certain sign of good times is the ability to say No. ~ Michael McNicholas

****

If you are not free to have a good time, you may as well go home. ~ Michael McNicholas

****

A mind is a terrific thing, it wanders all over the place. ~ Michael McNicholas

****

A lot of people don't want to be found. ~ Michael McNicholas

****

The only thing in life that comes equally every day is death. ~ Michael McNicholas

****

A bad man is a man without a heart. ~ Michael McNicholas

****

When you've lost all hope, the only thing that's left is to do your best. ~ Michael McNicholas

****

Remember that a lot of people are going to be thinking and saying things that will hurt you, and you can only control yourself. ~ Michael McNicholas

****

It's only by taking risks that we find out if we are really free. ~ Michael McNicholas

****

A lot of people want to be found. ~ Michael McNicholas

****

What may have been done in justice once can be done again. ~ Michael McNicholas

****

When it all comes down to it, who you are is way more important than what you have. ~ Michael McNicholas

****

Nobody can go back and start a new beginning, but anyone can start today and make a new ending. ~ Michael McNicholas

****

Redemption is a matter of completing the journey rather than the arrival. ~ Michael McNicholas

****

At times the only things people pay for with money are the things that money can't buy. ~ Michael McNicholas

****

The surest way to be content is to wish for what you have, is to wish to be content. For the secret of freedom lies in some such foolishness as that. We are all born of kings and beggars alike. ~ Henry Wadsworth Longfellow ~

****

Laugh at your problems, everybody else does. ~ Michael McNicholas

****

Freedom is a road never traveled. You have to seek it out. ~ Michael McNicholas

****

There is nothing worse than flaunting an achievement or flaunting a talent in front of somebody who doesn't have it. ~ Michael McNicholas

****

A commitment to something greater than self is a necessary piece of freedom. ~ Anonymous ~

****

The thing that lies at the foundation of positive thinking is the fact that you are going to do the best you can under the circumstances. ~ Michael McNicholas

****

Oftentimes you may get further with a kind word and a gun than you will with just a kind word. ~ Michael McNicholas

****

For the only thing worse than being looked down upon is not being looked up to. ~ Michael McNicholas

****

Freedom is never assured it has to be chosen every day. ~ Michael McNicholas

****

A lot of people are looking for doors that don't exist. ~ Michael McNicholas

****

It's not what we have in life, it's what we do with what we have. ~ Michael McNicholas

****

It is amazing how much can be done if no one cares who gets the credit. ~ Anonymous ~

*****

We can't become what we need to be by remaining what we are. ~ Henry David Thoreau ~

****

"It's not what happens to you in life that matters. It's what you do about it that really counts. ~ Henry David Thoreau ~

****

Do not be forever clasping your pearls to your bosom when you might be using them of to serve somebody else. ~ Golda Meir ~

****

Don't be too aggressive. Relax and be yourself and let the chips fall where they may. ~ Michael McNicholas

****

You have to carve the fireplace with the greatest care, but once you've done it you don't think about it again. ~ Michael McNicholas

*****

Everything that is great and remarkable in the world has been accomplished by people who have dared to be themselves. ~ Michael McNicholas

****

Make up your mind to turn the tables and play the game. ~ Ernest Hemingway ~

****

If you do not move forward the others will pass you by. ~ Michael McNicholas

****

If you don't like something stop doing it and then change it. ~ Michael McNicholas

****

You have to make the best of each and every moment in life, because in the blink of an eye it can be over. ~ Michael McNicholas

****

It is amazing how much can be done if no one cares who gets the credit. ~ Anonymous ~

****

No matter what happens, the important thing is that no one forgets. ~ Michael McNicholas

****

Do not worry about the future, or what may never be, but focus entirely on the present moment. ~ Alan Lakein ~

****

Stop me if you've heard this one before, the world is divided into cats who play well with others and cats who do not. I'm here to say that there's a remedy — do not play with others, you'll lose. ~ Michael McNicholas

****

If you don't want to be found do not get found. ~ Michael McNicholas

****

Your mission in life is to be, after receiving all you are capable of receiving, a blameless steward of that which remains. ~ Michael McNicholas

****

When one door closes another door opens. ~ Douglas Adams ~

****

When I am trying to achieve something of great importance to me, the first thing I do in the morning is tie up all the loose ends that are there. ~ Charles Schwab ~

November

People who are mindful all day long will be inclined to be mindful every minute of the day. ~ Michael McNicholas

****

It is not what happens to you in life that matters. It is what you do about it that really counts. ~ Henry David Thoreau ~

****

Looking at things too long is not the way to investigate them. ~ Henry David Thoreau ~

****

A man is known by the company he keeps. ~ Joseph Andrews ~

****

Fail often, fail often; fail better! ~ Michael McNicholas

****

Some people are ready to be free some people are ready to be free from themselves some people are not ready to be free ~ Michael McNicholas

****

A few per cent of the universe is ours to look after and it would be a pity if they let slip the opportunity. ~ Michael McNicholas

****

In matters of style, swim with the current; in matters of principle, stand like a rock. ~ Thomas Jefferson ~

****

The mind is like a parachute, it functions only when it is open. ~ Thomas Jefferson ~

****

We get to choose the way that we react to the events that happen to us. ~ Michael McNicholas

****

A commitment to something greater than self is a necessary piece of freedom. ~ Anonymous ~

****

The thing that lies at the foundation of positive thinking is the fact that you are going to do the best you can under the circumstances. ~ Michael McNicholas

****

If you are unnecessarily hard on yourself, people around you are unnecessarily hard on you. ~ Michael McNicholas

****

The greatest tragedy is not to die, but to feel that you have lived and lived for nothing. ~ Francois de La Rochefoucauld ~

****

There's always a bright side, even to the worst tragedy. ~ Michael McNicholas

****

Success is a poor man's refuge when the world mistakes him for being proud. ~ Michael McNicholas

****

The surest way to be content is to wish for what you have, is to wish to be content. For the secret of freedom lies in some such foolishness as that. We are all born of kings and beggars alike. ~ Henry Wadsworth Longfellow ~

****

Freedom is never assured it has to be chosen every day. ~ Michael McNicholas

****

A man is known by the company he keeps. ~ Joseph Andrews ~

****

The thing that lies at the foundation of positive thinking is the fact that you are going to do the best you can under the circumstances. ~ Michael McNicholas

****

A few per cent of the universe is ours to look after and it would be a pity if they let slip the opportunity. ~ Michael McNicholas

****

When everything seems to be going against you, remember that the airplane takes off against the wind, not with it. ~ Henry Ford ~

****

Freedom is never assured it has to be chosen every day. ~ Michael McNicholas ~

****

To enjoy the fruit of success you must first sow the seeds of determination. ~ Gregory H. Whitman ~

****

It is not what others get out of you, but what you get out of the experience that counts. ~ Harry Browne ~

****

Be more concerned with your character than with your reputation, because your character is what you really are, while your reputation is merely what others think you are. ~ Colin Cowherd ~

****

Reactions count for more than actions. ~ Colin Cowherd ~

****

You cannot climb a ladder unless you are willing to climb for the purpose of climbing the ladder. ~ Anthony J. D'Angelo ~

****

You are the person who you think you are, not the person others think you are. ~ Michael McNicholas

****

You may receive from others what they do to you, but you cannot give to others what they do not have in themselves. ~ Michael McNicholas

****

A bad man is a man without a heart. ~ Michael McNicholas

****

Hurry and use the moments which are given to you. ~ Michael McNicholas

****

The longest journey begins with a single step. ~ Michael McNicholas

****

Answer a fool according to his folly, lest he be wise in his own eyes. ~ Proverbs 26:5 ~

****

A heart that acts as a brake on the feet is bound to be trampled. ~ Michael McNicholas

****

Life is what happens while you are busy making other plans. ~ John Lennon ~

December

Freedom is a road never traveled. You have to seek it out. With every turn, you will find it different, because you are different. ~ Michael Basset

***

People often say that motivation doesn't last. Well, neither does bathing. That's why we recommend it daily. ~ Lazarus Long

***

Practice yourself, for heaven's sake, in little things; and thence proceed to greater. Never think from a great beginning. Think from a little beginning, and you will go on to a great end. ~ Francis William Newman

***

It is far better to be fond of humanity than to hate or be indiscriminate, even about our enemies. The object of hatred is to destroy, and indiscriminate hatred destroys more than it hurts; while that of love and care for our fellows is to help them and to place them on the way of better things. ~ William John Henry Boetcker

***

The same cowardice that makes our physical exertion vain, makes our intellectual exertion violent. ~ Phillips Brooks

***

I love this man. He is the genius of the century. His poetry is going to rank with Shakespeare and Chaucer and Milton. ~ Carl Sandburg

***

The highest ideal of man can never be attained, until we discover the true principle of self-government, which is that man can only be his own ruler, can only truly direct his own conduct, can only become great when he has within him the rule and regulation of his own soul. What is called great in man is not always greatness. In the noblest sense of the word, and as exemplified by Christ, greatness is the truest humility. ~ Richard Sibbes

***

Every man is the builder of a temple, called his body, to the god he worships, after a style purely his own, nor can he get off by hammering marble instead of living stones. ~ Henry David Thoreau

***

There is a wide difference between a strong-minded woman and a strong-minded man. A strong-minded man is apt to be a strong-bodied man; but a strong-minded woman is a contradiction in terms. ~ Quoted in Wit & Wisdom of the U. S. A. , compiled by Rossiter Johnson

***

You must do what you can with what you have, where you are. ~ Helen Keller

***

When you have rules, regulations, motives, yearnings, instincts, affections, a whimsicality, a wisdom of life that is separate from your education, then the years have indeed taught you their lesson and have gone, and you look back upon your life with the sorrow that comes to do ghosts of the dead. But when you exist from day to day on impulse and circumstance, then the years have taught you their lesson, and you look forward to a new and greater life to be lived. ~ E. M. Forster

***

The hardest thing in the world to understand is that when a man says he is a fool he usually means he is witty. ~ Voltaire

***

A man must be almost insane to write for the papers. ~ Mark Twain

***

A man is not idle because he is old or ill. No, he is happy because his interests and his work have become the same. He will hardly ever forget the labours of his life, if he is a thinker, if he follows truth for its own sake, for the great end of his life... He has remained faithful in what he has tried to do. He has lived his purpose all his life. He has forgotten nothing. He has lost nothing. Those things may have been unimportant... They were not. In his work he is still faithful. In his thought he is still faithful. This is what makes him content... Many people are helpless because they have never devoted themselves to anything which could not be accomplished by any perfectly healthy and normally developed person. ~ Carl Jung

***

It is only the good that steps forward. It is easy to be good, it is hard not to be good. ~ Alain Fournier Souvenirs Parteges

***

Resentment is like taking poison and hoping your enemies will die. ~ Nelson Mandela

***

I am too a Dreamer, dear Madam. — That in my dream shall walk a King, — A King whose voice shall ring through earth and sky, — While all men listen in silence! — Albert Edward, Prince of Wales, In "King Solomon" by Alfred Lord Tennyson

***

Let me make the songs of a nation, and I care not who writes its laws. ~ Robert Burns

***

You are born with grace. You need to find your truth. ~ Kunishige Yoshimura

***

Until you make the unconscious conscious, it will direct your life and you will call it fate. ~ Carl Jung

***

We are not wholly responsible for what we are or for what happens to us. The divide between the conscious and unconscious minds can have a lot to do with it. ~ Carl Jung

***

All education is based on a doubt as to what one does not know. ~ Johann Wolfgang von Goethe

***

I have met with more than one student who believes they are a failure because they don't share the belief system of the society they live in. I think that many of the problems with this society lie in the fact that it is based on belief in a "self-made man. " If people were educated to think of themselves as the result of factors outside themselves they would be more willing to become a part of a society in which they could contribute, rather than try to hold on to material and egocentric goals.

***

By wisdom the LORD laid the earth upon the waters: by understanding he created the heavens. ~ Proverbs 19:1

***

There is a single light of science, and to brighten it anywhere is to brighten it everywhere. ~ Edwin Powell Hubble

***

Music is the arithmetic of sounds as optics is the geometry of light. ~ Joseph-Louis Lagrange

***

A man may fall in the mud, but if he finds himself rebuilt, he has gained the universe. ~ Lebanese Proverb

***

All true art is one of the works of magic. ~ Eliphas Levi

***

The sun shines on all alike, and its rays call forth the gems that lie hidden in the earth. ~ Anonymous

***

A man who was completely innocent, offered himself as a sacrifice for the good of others, including his enemies, and became the ransom of the world. It was a perfect act. ~ Mahatma Gandhi

***

Good fences make good neighbors. ~ Robert Frost

***

The man who is prepared for misfortune will avoid it. ~ Samuel Johnson

***

Man usually arrives at his full stature in three stages: First as a child; then as a youth; last as a father. But greatness never arrives through a last stage. ~ Aristotle

***

God has not given man a measure of life but a breath of life. ~ Arabic Proverb

***.

Let your mistakes become your masters. ~ Homer

Bonus Quotes

You start to worry when you begin to see where people are going. ~ Jean Baudrillard

***

It's easier to move mountains than to change things in ourselves. ~ Abraham Lincoln

***

Regret is an emotion. Maybe a more active body's betrayal of the mind's trust in it is a betrayal of all passion. ~ J. B. Priestley

***

The universe is full of mysteries, and if you live long enough you realize that resolution of one mystery leads inevitably, if not directly, to resolution of another. ~ Isaac Asimov

***

We're not made tough by any accident of nature. It's something we have to work at; temperance and self-control. We have to endeavor not to fall below a certain level in our private lives. ~ Edward Abbey

***

The more disordered the house the heavier domestic obligations will be. ~ Aristotle

***

The rich are busy bodyguards of society, moving to defend it from the greed of the poor by the one weapon they have; money. ~ O. Henry

***

When the working man and his bosses both agree that the workers should get less, then, and only then the Depression is over. ~ Aneurin Bevan

***

How Muslims treat their women and children is a good indication of how women (and children) will be treated in the wider society. ~ Muhammad Ali

***

It is only in prosperity that people learn contentment with their lot. ~ J.B. Priestley

***

The poor are willing to be worse off for the sake of the rich being better off. ~ J. B. Priestley

***

After failure comes success. After defeat comes victory. Maybe it's a law. Maybe it's just the way it looks. ~ Robert McNamara

***

We are all responsible for what we are, for what we do. ~ Jacob Riis

***

All change is not change for the better. ~ Marshall McLuhan

***

Politics is not nobler than poetry. ~ J.B. Priestley

***

Most publishers want you to write something sexy. They would like to go to bed with you. They dream about you. They want to be close to you. They want to do it. They will take you in the most delightful way. Then you'll want to do it to them in the most delightful way. That is the way authors write. They always fall in love. They always have sex. They even become engaged to their publishers. Why not? The more people you know, the more you read. It's emotional. It's drug-induced.

~ Gloria Mark

***

I regard struggle as the central fact of my life. Struggle influenced my choice of books. It gave my life direction and the feeling of dignity which is the essential ingredient in all forms of self-respect and self-confidence.

~ Joseph Leftwich

***

I've always said, if you do what you love and you're good at it, then you'll never work a day in your life.

~ Oprah Winfrey

***

I accept the responsibilities of life as they come, not as they were meant to be. ~ Mary Call Guinn

***

We are not responsible for the evil in us. But by self-discipline we can conquer that which is evil in others. ~ Luther Burbank

***

A lot of people never learn how to be still. ~ Storm Purvis

Choose not to do – that is one of the things that can make you love yourself. ~ George Bernard Shaw

***

There is a perpetual struggle between the past and the present. We want to preserve the memory of the past without being constrained by it; we want to strive forward, we want to gain all the values that a new age and a new country have to offer us, without who knows what absurdities or mistakes of the past that we cannot share. ~ Jean-Paul Sartre

***

It is glorious to learn from your mistakes... but not if too many memories of them are destroyed in the process. ~ Andrew Sevier Jr.

***

We commit the noblest of all sins by underestimating our real strength. ~ William Feather

***

Your parents do not give you life. They merely prepare you for some of its situations. ~Eleanor Roosevelt

***

I am big, I contain multitudes a simple inventory of my mind or my life would stretch beyond the current limits of the universe. ~Christopher Kelly

***

If you want to succeed in life, focus on accomplishing your dreams, not on achieving your goals. ~ Andrew Sevier Jr.

***

Don't waste time solving problems you don't have.

Appreciate the freedom problems free you from.

-Author Unknown

***

He loved her. Not so much because she was beautiful and wondering, but because she was smart and willing to allow him to be smart, and because of the way her eyes, so alive in their deep sea blue, burned suddenly when she deviated from, or really accepted, reality. ~ J.K. Rowling

We have been planted just like a tree, by the Master Care Taker. God, gave him that right, to take care of us, because he is the only one...who really cares. All the things we do, what is the use? If we don't have God, what good thing will we do? ~ J.K. Rowling

***

We are here to seek joy, we are here to seek peace, to seek the happiness that transcends understanding, a joy that cannot be described. ~ Dalai Lama XIV

***

Only the foolish and cowardly need fear death; everyone else should glory in it. ~Death is only the great equalizer. It eliminates all pride and prejudice. ~Charles de Margerie

***

Better to be something than to seem like everything. ~ Andrew Sevier Jr.

***

If you help enough people, you will have helped many lifetimes. ~ Andrew Sevier Jr.

***

A man's true, his only friend is time. ~ Unknown

***

Even mountains will crumble before this invincible force, but what will remain is our humility and our love.

~Unknown

***

Do what you can. With what you have. Where you are. ~ Theodore Roosevelt

***

I'm going to be alone. I'm going to make mistakes. I'm going to hurt myself. I will make messes. But you're not going to hurt me. You're not going to leave me. You're not going to stop loving me. ~ Jodi Picoult

***

A strong tree is known for its quiet. A weak tree is known for its silence. ~Author Unknown

***

If you can't make it right, you can't make it wrong. ~ Andrew Sevier Jr.

***

Take away my fear of death. I desire to understand everything. I desire to know the meaning of life, of suffering, of pain, of pleasure. There may be many answers, but each answer is a piece of the puzzle, a way to love unconditionally. The joy will come when no one has to suffer, when no one has to cry. ~ Andrew Sevier Jr.

***

Is the human mind the problem or the solution? ~ Andrew Sevier Jr.

***

I cannot always do as I would; but I can do as I must. ~ William Shakespeare

***

"If we can't spend the same, can we still love each other?"

"Of course!" ~ Andrew Sevier Jr.

***

In one hundred years time science will have discovered immortality but not human relationships. ~ Ken Wilber

***

Learn about people by studying their work, not their lives. ~ Andrew Sevier Jr.

***

It requires no great courage to stand up to your enemies, it requires great wisdom to stand up to your friends. ~ Mahatma Gandhi

***

The aim of Science is to solve problems; the aim of Literature is to find them. ~ Albert Einstein

***

A change is gonna come. ~ Sam Cooke

***

The best moment to plant a tree is now. The second best moment is right now. ~ Chinese Proverb

***

If you want to be amazing, be accepting of all amazing things around you. ~ Andrew Sevier Jr.

***

Stubbornness can be overcome by a beaten horse but not by a beaten dog. ~ Unknown

***

There are two ways to live your life: first, as if nothing is a miracle. Then as if everything is. ~ Albert Einstein

***

To give generously is good, but to give without end is worthless. ~ Su Dongpo

***

The only way to hurt the master is to kill yourself. ~Author Unknown

***

If you don't feel happy, it is because you aren't happy with yourself. ~ Author Unknown

***

It is a mathematical fact that the most perfect straight line is an extension of the most perfect circle. ~ Author Unknown

***

The great secret of happiness is to restrain desire, and to wait without hope. ~ William Blake

***

Men can't live by bread alone. ~ Amy Grant

***

In every life there comes a moment to decide. And the decision is yours. ~ Andrew Sevier Jr.

***

The measure of our success is the roots we go into the ground. ~ Andrew Sevier Jr.

***

If life could be more like writing a story, we would be able to change it any moment. ~ Andrew Sevier Jr.

***

The most important things aren't things. ~ Andrew Sevier Jr.

***

We believe in a God who not only makes the rain fall on the just and the unjust, but who, right now, is sending sweet rain to grow seeds for planting in the spring. ~ John Green

***

If you help enough people, you will have helped many lifetimes. ~ Andrew Sevier Jr.

***

A man's true, his only friend is time. ~ Unknown

***

Power increases proportionally to the need to control. ~ Unknown

***

We send them far away, into the future, and one by one, we close our eyes and sit by our death beds and wait for the kiss that never comes. ~ Andrew Sevier Jr.

***

Let your worries fall like rain drops into the ocean of your knowledge. And let your prayers take rise like the sun from the deep ocean of your wisdom. ~ Andrew Sevier Jr.

***

Theories are the only things I know to be true, but I don't know how true they are. ~ Andrew Sevier Jr.

***

Fire can be controlled. It can be extinguished. But cannot be truly destroyed. ~ Author Unknown

***

Maybe what we love the most lasts only a little while, but it always leaves a trace behind. ~ Andrea Castillo

***

What IS right will always eventually triumph. What IS wrong will always eventually fail. ~ Andrew Sevier Jr.

***

The most measure of control you have, the least control you will ever feel. ~ Andrew Sevier Jr.

***

How do you tell a child that he is beloved before he even understood the question? ~Elise Cope

***

When you wait for love, you lose it. When you run after it, you lose your track. ~ Elisabeth Kubler-Ross

***

I will only bother you when I need you. I will only love you when I can. And only when I am able. ~ Andrew Sevier Jr.

***

All you need is love. But only a little. ~ Erich FROMM

***

We really don't need to learn something new every day. We only need to spend a few minutes to discover some thing we are capable of doing, doing it right now. ~Andrew Sevier Jr.

***

A committee is a cul de sac down which ideas are lured and quietly strangled. ~ Robin Skynner

***

We want the facts...yes; but we want someone to make us feel the facts. ~ George Bernard Shaw

***

We are justified in spending a lifetime in becoming the persons we are. ~ Martin Luther King, Jr.

***

It is especially important to stretch tight muscles; to become aware of taking the easy way out; of doing what is comfortable and secure; of avoiding new challenges. ~ F. David Peat

***

Maturity is anabilomy, not a date on a calendar. ~ M. Scott Peck

***

Once you have faced your fear, you win. ~ Eckhart Tolle

***

They say the most useless person can organize a successful meeting. ~ Patton

***

If only one person could understand his message, you would be all-powerful. ~ Carl Jung

***

Some people are too bold to shine. ~ L.M. Hart

***

A big-hearted person who does something kind for you doesn't hurt you. But a mean person who does something kind for you hurts a lot. ~ Author Unknown

***

Loving someone is unpopular, but it sure as hell beats hating someone. ~ Author Unknown

***

Spare the rod, spoil the child. ~ Proverbs

***

Tell the truth. If your bitter, be honest. ~ Yvonne Nelson

***

Hidden inside you, a million dreams are waiting to be born. ~ unknown

***

The person who has nothing to say will say it anyway, and will continue to say it until he's exhausted himself or, very often, until the listeners are exhausted. ~ Gustave Flaubert

***

It is a common saying in the army that an officer knows less and less about his men the longer he is up. ~ O.V. Kuzyk

***

The best ideas come as jokes. Make your thinking as funny as possible. ~ Richard P. Feynman

***

What that which we call a rose, but which is called a rose by no one, is to the full-blown flower itself. ~ David Hume

***

The strangest artist is man. He is never nature's greatest artist, for he is taken by surprise; nor naturalistic artist, for he follows after his model blindly; nor is he, therefore, the highest, for he is without motive. He, therefore, is man, that is, the accidental, the improbable. ~ Hermann Hesse

***

If success is what you want, you have not chosen the right way. ~ Helen Keller

***

The long road to success is the main thing in the life of man. ~ Richard Nixon

***

Too many of us concentrate so much of our lives on the things we hope or fear will never happen that we fail to have any life at all. ~ Helen Hayes

***

The best kind of friend is the kind that I have never seen and never will. The kind you show to your children and pass on to your grandchildren. ~ Author Unknown

***

If you are doing your best, you will not have time to worry about failure. ~ Tammy Dray

***

If you make life too easy for yourself it beats two ways. ~ Samson F. Hoiles

***

An idea would be worth the most if it came to life through one's own efforts. Those who have not made their ideas move not can not have them. ~ Unknown

***

It's easy to grow up. I had a good teacher. ~ Author Unknown

***

It's not whether you get knocked down. It's whether you get up. ~ Author Unknown

***

The measure of a person is how they react to adversity. ~ Michael Graves

***

It is astonishing how many people are talking without doing. ~ Ethan Allen Hitchcock

***

The force of imagination is greater than all other forces. ~ Albert Einstein

***

Most so-called problems are opportunities in disguise. ~ Fred Allen

***

The problems you encounter late will never make you appear late. ~ Anonymous

***

There are no accidents. There is only cause and effect. ~ Lao Tzu

***

The best revenge is massive success. ~ Frank Sinatra

***

More things are lost on the road to success than the road to failure. ~ Deng Xiaoping

***

Real weapons are always the best for winning real battles. ~ Sun Tzu

***

The hardest habit to break is believing you can't. ~ Anthony Liccione

***

Nothing breeds more contempt in a home than an overly critical father and a nagging mother. ~ Unknown

***

Our best thoughts come from others. ~ Johann Wolfgang von Goethe

***

Each of our problems presents us with an opportunity to improve our skills. ~ Anthony Liccione

Nothing breeds more contempt in a home than an overly critical father and a nagging mother. ~ Unknown

***

You make so many crazy things, you need a safe place to store them. It's called your imagination. ~ Reese Witherspoon

***

A person with a great deal of talent is capable of forgetting how to use it. ~ Truman Capote

***

When all is said and done, the toughest battle we fight in life comes from the battle of trying to relax. ~ Charles R. Swindoll

***

What the wise men are searching for is not a answer, it is a question. ~ George Bernard Shaw

***

It's not true you know, all that stuff, about girls, and crying. As if. ~ Richard

***

Lessons are to be learned when you have to do them yourself. ~ Anthony Liccione

***

The key to success is to grow faster than your competition, but never to outgrow your market's capacity to absorb the output. ~ J. S. Marcus

***

It is most difficult to see one's own faults. ~ H.G. Wells

***

Don't worry about people stealing an idea and stealing your success. Instead worry about people making an idea bigger than yours. ~ Unknown

***

Most men dream of hours they wish they had in a day. ~ Etienne de la Boëtie

***

If you live outside the lines, there's no line to live by. ~ Kenny Rogers

***

You can never really know anything for sure, but you must try anyway. ~ Katherine Mansfield

***

Not for one moment do I lose sight of the fact that behind my success stands the name Webster Military High School, and behind Webster Military High School stands you, the patron. ~ Neil G. McFadyen

***

Happiness is the antithesis of risk. ~ Otto von Bismarck

***

Life is a work of art. ~ William James

***

The only thing I fear in the future is fear. ~ Alexander Graham Bell

***

When you make a mistake you pay for it every day, every hour, every moment of your life. ~ Lyndon B. Johnson

***

If you sacrifice your values, your dreams will surely die. ~ Unknown

***

Work hard everyday. Follow your heart, then listen to that little voice that will tell you when to stop. ~ Author Unknown

***

Forgive yourself the things you didn't make and try to forget the ones you did. ~ Unknown

***

You can make sure of two things in life: that success will not come unlooked for and that you will have no regrets for not having tried. ~ Arthur Conan Doyle

If you think you are too small to make a difference, try sleeping with a mosquito. ~ Author unknown.

***

Some people mistake a short memory for a clear conscience. ~ Richard M. Nixon

***

Never lose sight of the fact that the majority of people in the world hate you, and are trying to destroy you. ~ Alan W. Watts

***

A successful person in business gets up in the morning and goes to bed at night with questions in his mind. ~ Donald Trump

***

A great deal of failure is due to unchecked self-confidence. ~ Thomas Fuller

***

It's no good looking back at trouble and thinking 'I could have done better.' You can't do better; you did your best and have to live with that. ~ Terry Pratchett

***

Winners take risks; losers don't. ~ Charles Schwab

Look at comfort and see that you are merely adding one more thing to your problem. ~ Thomas Stockdill

***

Forgive yourself for your faults; it's not hard, and you will have a wonderful chance to begin again. ~ Frances H. Underwood

***

There is no such thing as failure. If you aim at nothing you will surely hit it. ~ Samuel Butler

***

Everyone sees what they want to see. ~ Plato

***

What we need is more confidence. ~ Anthony Liccione

***

When your parents are gone, you simply can't choose your parents if you want to keep your mental health, instead just love them. ~ James C. Webb Jr.

***

Don't cry because it's over. Smile because it happened. ~ Dr. Seuss

***

When I doubt, I have a fool for a friend. ~ Robert Browning

You can't ever do anything alone. I'm not doing this alone. I've got some help, and so have you. ~ Jim Valvano

***

Don't let the world and its troubles get you down. Just remember, one day at a time, the sun will come out, the rain will stop, and you'll be back in business. ~ Paul Harvey

***

Do not be afraid of making mistakes. You are afraid of one only if you mistake what you can do. ~ George Herbert

***

You can make more enemies by kindness than by harshness. ~ Epictetus

***

We must learn to labor and win success even if we must sacrifice happiness with the result. ~ Douglas MacArthur

***

You won't always be right. Become wrong enough often enough, and eventually, something right will figure itself out. ~ J. C. Webb Jr.

***

Don't be afraid of failure. Be afraid of not trying. ~ Unknown

***

You see, even God made mistakes. He even killed His own son. ~ Esther Earl

Don't let the world make you the way you are. Be the person you want to be. ~ Ernest Hemingway

***

Silence is the best thing a destroyer of dreams can possess, for it has a strong virtue and a tender power. ~ St. Augustine

***

What is done in love is done by the lover, not by her subject. ~ Rumi

***

It is the aim of the wise man to make things easy for the ignorant. ~ Baltasar Gracian

***

Letters are the muscles of the mind. Opening them is like exercising them. ~ Niel Gaiman

***

If you don't faint on the first hill, you'll definitely crawl on the last. ~ Unknown

***

If you stop toying with something, you may get it. ~ Chinese Proverb

***

Too much learning is almost as bad as not enough. ~ Unknown

Grace is the most beautiful gift I have ever received. It is a gift of love that saved me from self-imposed guilt. ~ Nature's Crysmutopia

***

The dreams we give up come back transformed into reality. ~ Jean Jacques Rousseau

***

Above all things, never lie to yourself. The man who never lies to himself can be other things to others; but no one else can be lie to him- -all others, even the best of them, are possible to him only on their own terms, and he can meet with no possibility of consolation or assistance from them. ~ Charles Darwin

***

You don't find the bad guys, you make them. ~ Joseph Conrad

***

There are two types of optimists: the group of people who can always see the good in other people, and the group of people who are fooling themselves. ~ Patricia T. O'Conner

***

The art of being wise is the art of recognizing what is evil. ~ Plato

***

Chase your dreams. Live your dreams. You're not as good as you can be, but you're not as bad as you can be. ~ : Ocean Hart

Life isn't about finding yourself, it's about creating yourself. ~ George Bernard Shaw

***

Always go on in the way that seems best to you. And when you have doubts, don't hesitate to ask for advice. Ask as many people as you like. But follow your own feelings, too. The only reason not to follow your heart is because you're afraid you might get hurt. But, then again, you already know that is true. So what else can you expect? ~ Stevie Wonder

***

Only the shallow know more than they show. ~ Brian Clough

***

You have enemies? Good. That means you've stood up for something, sometime in your life.

~ Winston Churchill

***

Mankind neither desires war nor engages in it without motive, without hope or fear.– Leo Tolstoy

***

Most people choose unhappiness in the long run. ~ Eric Hoffer

One of the most important things I've learned over the years is to be happy with what you have. Be happy with what you've got and use it in such a way that your life reflects what you have. ~ Denzel Washington

***

You don't have a soul. You are a Soul. You have a body. ~ C.S. Lewis

***

You did not die for me, or for any man, you died for yourself. You were tired and sick of the world and did not want to leave it, and now you are much happier not being here. ~ Edward R. Murrow

***

Be warned, whenever we're feeling cynical and sarcastic, we're getting close to the truth. ~ Joseph P. Riley

***

I've found at times like this it's good to remember that there have always been times like this. ~ Arthur Schlesinger, Jr.

***

Love is what happens to a man and woman who don't know each other well enough. ~ Karen Blixen

***

Pessimism is ignorance, and optimism is prejudice. ~ Albert Camus

***

The price of greatness is responsibility. ~ Winston Churchill

There is nothing new in life. There are no new landscapes, no new faces, no new feelings. What we experience has all happened before. ~ S.D. Gordon

***

"I am fond of pigs. Dogs look up to us. Cats look down on us. Pigs treat us as equals." ~ Winston Churchill

***

"A long-range bomber can ruin your day. A short-range rifleman can ruin your life." ~ Colonel Joseph Dunford

***

The number of legs a man has is not indicative of how many times he can fall down. ~ Doug Larson

***

"Murdering is a crime, but using means that are designed to kill is a means." ~ N.C. Wyeth

***

When we die, we die alone. That's the worst part of it. What's essential is that we remember with gratitude the things we lived for. ~ William Butler Yeats

***

"When you have no future, you make the best of today." ~ J. Hawthorne

I go fishing alone and often. It helps me to think, and more than anything else, I need to think. ~ Henry David Thoreau

***

Impossible means I'm possible. ~ Pablo Picasso

***

If you are walking down the right path and you are willing to keep walking, eventually you will make progress. ~ Barack Obama

***

"Fortune favors the bold." ~ Shakespeare

***

"There's always a chance if you're going into battle. Are you sure you want to win?" ~ Winston Churchill

***

"I have knocked my brains out with the piano and that makes me feel better." ~ Cole Porter

***

As you make your journey through life, don't look back and ask yourself if you've made mistakes. Look back and ask yourself if you've learned. ~ Rosalynn Carter

***

"My definition of an optimist is someone who believes that this is the best of all possible worlds." ~ Anatole France

"There's a carriage, a horse and four,

The coachman mounts the box, and the children on the way." ~ Edward Lear

***

"A man may be as great as he chooses, if he will sacrifice everything else to the one great aim." ~ Orison Swett Marden

***

"My grandparents were immigrants and my grandparents were cooks." ~ Tom Hanks

***

"One of the greatest casualties of the war in Vietnam has been the Great Society... shot down on the battlefield of Vietnam." ~ Hubert Humphrey

***

"It is a hundred times better to have common sense without education than to have education without common sense." ~ Robert G.

***

The world is yours. Your task is to take it. ~ Oliver Wendell Holmes

***

I'm not getting up just to place another bet. ~ Erin Dilly

All big accomplishment start with the decision to try. ~ Meg Rowley

***

Enthusiasm is contagious. ~ Calvin Coolidge

***

Don't quit just because you can't figure out everything right now. The real answers will come to you. ~ Dave Ramsey

***

A healthy spirit can bear a great deal of trouble. ~ Ralph Waldo Emerson

***

If you want to go fast, go alone, if you want to go far, go together. ~ African Proverb

***

There is a big difference between knowing the way out and knowing the way. ~ Henry James

***

If the way out is known, there is no point walking. ~ Confucius

***

If you wish to see the unseen, open your eyes and look around you. ~ Rumi

When you see someone act with courage, you just have a harder time not acting the same way. ~ Ryan Holiday

***

To make a great demand upon life, we must make a great demand upon ourselves. ~ William Ellery Channing

***

A great way to improve anything is to start it anew. ~ Ralph Waldo Emerson

***

The man who refuses to rise when he can't is not fit to rise. ~ Abraham Lincoln

***

Courage is nothing else than justice metamorphosed into will. ~ Oliver Wendell Holmes

***

A little imagination is a dangerous thing, and dreams are hopeless without it. ~ William Blake

***

My key to success is positive thinking – the ability to think and feel what you would like to happen, without doubt and without fear. ~ Robert Collier

Our happiness is the aim of our existence, and not a means to any end. ~ Aristotle

***

No one need wait a single moment before starting to improve the world. ~ Anne Frank

***

What would life be if we had no courage to attempt anything? ~ Vincent Van Gogh

***

Do what you can, where you are, with what you have. ~ Theodore Roosevelt

***

Courageous living requires we take action in the face of our fears, not run from them. ~ Robert T. Kiyosaki

***

Avoid idle speculation and vain dreaming. Live rather, and stoop to conquer. ~ Robert Louis Stevenson

December
***
Never, never, never give up. ~ Winston Churchill

***

You can't move forward without moving backward. ~ Alan Cohen

In order to have happiness in life, you need to have gratitude in life.

***

The ability to meet trouble head on and turn it into something good can make all the difference in the world.

***

We are the sum of our choices. ~ Dalai Lama

***

We should never fear the loss of life's little pleasures, for no matter how short life, there are enough pleasures in it to make it worth living. ~ Aung San Suu Kyi

***

If you don't build your dreams, someone else will hire people to do it for you. ~ Michael Dell

***

Time waits for no one... A pessimist complains about the wind; an optimist expects it to change; a realist adjusts the sails. ~ William A. Ward

***

Motivation is your friend or your enemy. It fuels you into action – or saps you of power and leaves you floundering. ~ Harvey Mackay

Attitude is an expression of your soul at any given moment. ~ Victor Frankl

***

There is a reason why people crack under pressure. Its not because your pressure... it's because you don't have the ability to think clearly. ~ Mark Cuban

***

Some people never go through hell,

till they become angels. ~ William Blake

***

When you tell yourself you're not good enough, you're right. ~ Dr. Phil

***

Don't quit... just grow up. ~ Craig Kilborn

***

Long after we are gone the echoes of our lives will ring in the hearts of those who love us, and the world will have to express a respect for the story of their lives as much as it did for the story of their deaths. ~ Elizabeth George

***

Dying isn't the hardest thing. Living when you know deep down that you're too fucked up to be saved... that's the hardest thing. ~ Chuck Palahniuk

Good or bad the outcome is in your hands. ~ Ebenezer Scrooge

***

The cure for boredom is curiosity. ~ Eric Hoffer

***

It may be the most beautiful thing that you have ever experienced in your life, to realise that you are one of the important people in the universe. It's the most painful. · ~ R. Buckminster Fuller

***

Because we fail we must try again. Because we suffer we must heal. Because we grieve we must love. And because we die we must live. ~ Jody Turner

***

You can't hide the truth of pain, even if you cover it with other feelings. But you can reveal its truth by showing your heart's endurance in your life, and that is what makes the difference between being resilient and being broken. ~ Shannon L. Alder

***

Do or do not. There is no try. ~ Master Yoda

***

To have a great relationship, you need to ask two questions: 1. Are we happy with who we are? 2. Are we happy with how we treat each other? If you can answer yes to both, you are on your way. ~ Chad Ochocinco

Joy often comes to those who seek it most earnestly. ~ Ralph Waldo Emerson

***

I find the optimist wasting time is a sad travesty of existence. The pessimist is an ambitious failure. What a joke. ~ Dan Rather

***

We didn't start hunting buffalo to protect them, we started hunting buffalo to eat them. ~ Daniel Kilgard

***

A decision to act comes when appreciation for the opportunity to act becomes strong enough to override fear of failure. ~ Christopher Alexander

***

When you can see the value of obvious things you see clearly for the first time. ~ Bern Keatings

***

Altruism is the only way to be happy. ~ Richard Bach

***

Those who don't change become extinct. ~ Peter F. Drucker

***

The symbol of hope in an individual's life is a commitment that starts with I am and turns into we are. ~ Harvey Mackay

***

It is widely held – and it is a mistake – that people don't change. A successful person who is a good manager or supervisor, a good lover or a good parent is often the same person in the third decade as in the first. The last twenty years can make little or no difference, since the core of the person remains intact. ~ Marion Power

***

It's not what happens to you – it's what you do with what happens to you. ~ Zig Ziglar

***

Those who see the beauty of the world will never seek the ugly side of life. ~ Shunryu Suzuki Roshi

***

I don't see much sense in having compassion for a tigerskin rug. ~ Hunter S. Thompson

***

Never say die, never give up. ~ Nelson Mandela

***

I think failure is like rejection. You get used to it. You get over it. Things don't mean anything until you make them mean something. ~ Bo Jackson

We must go beyond the troubled generation and choose to live a life of purpose, of making a difference, of giving, of curiosity, of purpose, of hope, of dreams, of faith. ~ Barack Obama

***

We learn from failure even more than we do from success. So, learn from setbacks, and learn from courage. ~ Garry Kasparov

***

Freakish accidents that destroy the physical career that demanded a lifetime of sacrifice can crush the most manly soul. ~ Christopher Reeve

***

The potential to change comes from the ability to admit that there is a problem. ~ Christopher Reeve

***

Talent is God given. Be humble therefore with willingness to learn... Great talent instantly translates into visible results. ~ Tony Sterio

***

Hope is a good thing – maybe the best of things, and no good thing ever dies. ~ Andy Dufresne (Tom Hanks) in The Shawshank Redemption

***

The Supreme Art of Learning is the Art of Learning to Learn. ~ John Henry Newman

***

It's never too late to be what you might have been. ~ George Elliot

***

Sometimes it's every fool for himself. ~ Richard Bach

***

The future only happens once. There's no use worrying about it, because it'll always happen to somebody else. ~ Richard Bach

***

Don't delay, the chance may never come. ~ William Shakespeare

***

Excuses are good when they work, but not when they don't work. ~ Iris Barry

***

The true measure of one's success is the kind of life they were able to leave behind. ~ Iris Barry

***

One way or another, the path I walked was my own. ~ Richard Feynman

***

The cure for boredom is curiosity. There is no cure for curiosity. ~ Alice Bailey

The best example I can set is to live a life of compassion. ~ Dalai Lama XIV

***

The only way out is through. ~ Robert A. Heinlein

***

To quote Shakespeare, "A strange thing is happening here. People who don't know what they're doing are doing it so well." ~ E. O. Wilson

***

Give up thinking and start acting. ~ Eckhart Toleman

***

Disappointment is the keystone of tragedy because 'disappointment is the keystone of hope.' ~ William Butler Yeats

***

The good life is one inspired and nourished by counsel and encouragement. ~ Marcus Aurelius

***

The most terrible things that we hear daily have not really happened. ~ Marcus Aurelius

***

The main point is not to waste time, but to enjoy it. ~ Frangoise Sagan

***

Zesty are our wishes, yet to give them wing is dearer far than all the fowl of the air. ~ Pindar

***

My greatest strength: common sense; my greatest weakness: assuming that common sense will be common between men. ~ Albert Einstein

***

What distinguishes the hard-boiled detective from other fictional detectives is his sense of social responsibility. The detective, on a long-term investigation, never forgets he was sent to the police to protect citizens, that his conscience is clear, and that he was involved in an honorable, honorable profession. ~ Sir Arthur Conan Doyle

***

Interaction, not vice versa, is the driving force of the universe. ~ Arnold Steinhardt

***

The blue train deposited Collins on the edge of the river. Within seconds its identity was lost in the rustling of the autumnal foliage. ~ The Hunt for Red October

***

It's not how many times you fall down, it's how many times you get back up that counts. ~ Joel Garfinkle

***

I discovered that if you want something said, ask a man; if you want something done, ask a woman. ~ Margaret Thatcher

***

We must believe in luck. For when we believe in ourselves, we become capable of anything. ~ Rudyard Kipling

***

Life is a miracle, but people do not want to believe that it is so. ~ Jonas Salk

***

Sometimes things do not change. ~ Jonas Salk

***

Progress is impossible without continual change-for everything becomes old. ~ Mary Colum

***

People don't think of change as being necessary, because they associate change with pain. ~ Satyajit Ray

***

I have discovered that in nothing do men more deceive themselves than in the way they treat their own passions. ~ Montaigne

If you progress, good things will be awarded to you and you will have nothing to regret. ~ Sun Tzu

***

One of the finest qualities of true friendship is to understand and to be understood. ~ Samuel Taylor Coleridge

***

People don't seem to realize that you can't make a joke without telling the truth. ~ Sam Levenson

***

We've made some mistakes, but we're not dummies. ~ Ronald Reagan

***

Water, taken in moderation, cannot hurt anybody. ~ Benjamin Franklin

***

As long as I can hear the grand music of creation, I am happy with what I've become and where I've been. ~ William Beebe

***

The reason so many women have short tempers is that they lack the tool they need to manage their anger. ~ Hanna Segal

***

I prefer lemons to oranges because lemons are sour and oranges are sweet. ~ Ambros Gulbe

Seeing is believing. No seeing, no believing. ~ Ambros Gulbe

***

There's no total in the universe. ~ Evelyn Glennie

***

Happiness and health are two things you can have for the asking; sorrow comes along at the most inconvenient moments. ~ B.R. Ambedkar

***

The best of all possible worlds depends on the observer. ~ Jasper Morello

***

Don't count the days, make the days count. ~ Jasper Morello

***

He who paints his own life dies. ~ Thomas TenBerge

***

To have done anything just for money or for applause is a mistake that I will never be guilty of again. ~ Maud Van Doren

***

The world is full of people having a wonderful time. ~ Ebenezer Henderson

God lets trials come through friends, rather than arbitrarily dealing with us through the terrible events of nature. We are given relationships like a plant is given sunlight and water. ~ Rory Peck

***

Nobody's perfect. Therefore, I am happy. ~ Rory Peck

***

I live to know that I am intending to live. ~ Socrates

***

I am astonished by the ease with which I slipped into the little absurdities of daily life; it is a matter of habit, I suppose. ~ Andre Gide

***

You have to be kind of quiet inside to resists the temptation. ~ Ernest Hemingway

***

A woman should be loved as she deserves, but not for what she deserves. ~ Karl XII

***

Disaster! is just a word to a man with nothing more. ~ Longfellow

***

The strength of a man is his fullness of life. ~ Albert Schweitzer

***

Life can only be understood backward. But it must be lived forwards.

www.ingramcontent.com/pod-product-compliance
Lightning Source LLC
Chambersburg PA
CBHW071526080526
44588CB00011B/1565